My
Senses
SMELLING

by
Grace Jones

Words written in **yellow** are explained in the glossary on page 24.

CONTENTS

PAGE 4–5   What are My Senses?

PAGE 6–9   How do I Smell?

PAGE 10–11   Smells

PAGE 12–13   Near and Far

PAGE 14–15   In the Kitchen

PAGE 16–17   In the Garden

PAGE 18–19   Staying Safe

PAGE 20–21   Super Senses!

PAGE 22–23   What can you Smell?

PAGE 24   Index and Glossary

©2016
Book Life
King's Lynn
Norfolk PE30 4LS

ISBN: 978-1-910512-67-8

Written by:
Grace Jones
Edited by:
Gemma McMullen
Designed by:
Drue Rintoul

A catalogue record for this book
is available from the British Library.

WHAT ARE MY SENSES?

We all have 5 **senses**. They are sight, smell, taste, touch and hearing.

Your senses tell you what is going on around you.

HOW DO I SMELL?

NOSE

You use your nose to help you to smell.

You breathe in air through your nose.

NOSE

BRAIN

Special parts of your nose
send messages to your brain.

Your brain tells you what you are smelling.

SMELLS

There are many different sorts of smells in the world.

LEMONS HAVE A STRONG SCENT.

Some things have a strong **scent** and others have a very weak scent.

11

NEAR AND FAR

If an object is far away,
it takes longer for you to smell it.

If it is near to you, you can smell it more quickly.

COOKIES

Some foods smell so good that it makes you want to eat them.

Other foods have strong smells
that might stop you from eating them.

IN THE GARDEN

In the spring and summer, you can smell the scent of some flowers.

The grass in your garden has a particular smell when it is cut.

Your sense of smell can tell you when you are in danger.

When you smell smoke, your brain tells you something is **burning**.

SUPER SENSES!

ANTENNAE

BUTTERFLY

Butterflies use their antennae to smell with, just like we use our noses.

They use them to find food
that smells good.

WHAT CAN YOU SMELL?

Ask an adult to find three foods with strong smells. Close your eyes and smell each of the foods.

Can you guess what each of the foods are?
What does each one smell like?

GLOSSARY

ANTENNAE
two long thin parts found on an insect.

BRAIN
tells your body what to do.

BURNING
on fire.

SCENT
the smell of something.

SENSES
tell you what is going
on around you.

INDEX

BUTTERFLY 20, 21
FOOD 14, 15, 21, 22, 23
GARDEN 16, 17
KITCHEN 14, 15
NOSE 6, 7, 8, 18, 22
SENSES 4, 5, 18
SMELL 4, 6, 9, 10, 11, 12, 13, 16, 19, 20,
          21, 22, 23

24